loveamore

This is the story of Paddy Hannan.

Written by Esme Kent.

The pamphlet was illustrated in 1988 by artist Warren Gundry.

The pamphlet was sold in the Kalgoorlie between 1988 and 1994 and is now re-released in 2021 in book format.

THE
STORY OF
PADDY HANNAN

BY ESME KENT

ILLUSTRATIONS BY WARREN GUNDRY

loveamore

Paddy Hannan sits,
in bronze upon the street,
watching folk rush by,
with heavy tramping feet.
His waterbag lays tilted,
his pick axe stands close by,
and Paddy seems to sit there,
with a thoughtful look in eye.

Naman Gurty

Perhaps he is looking back,

to a time long since gone,

about the hardships in the outback,

when the search for gold was on.

And how the lack of water,

could drive a man insane,

beneath a blazing sun,

without a sign of rain.

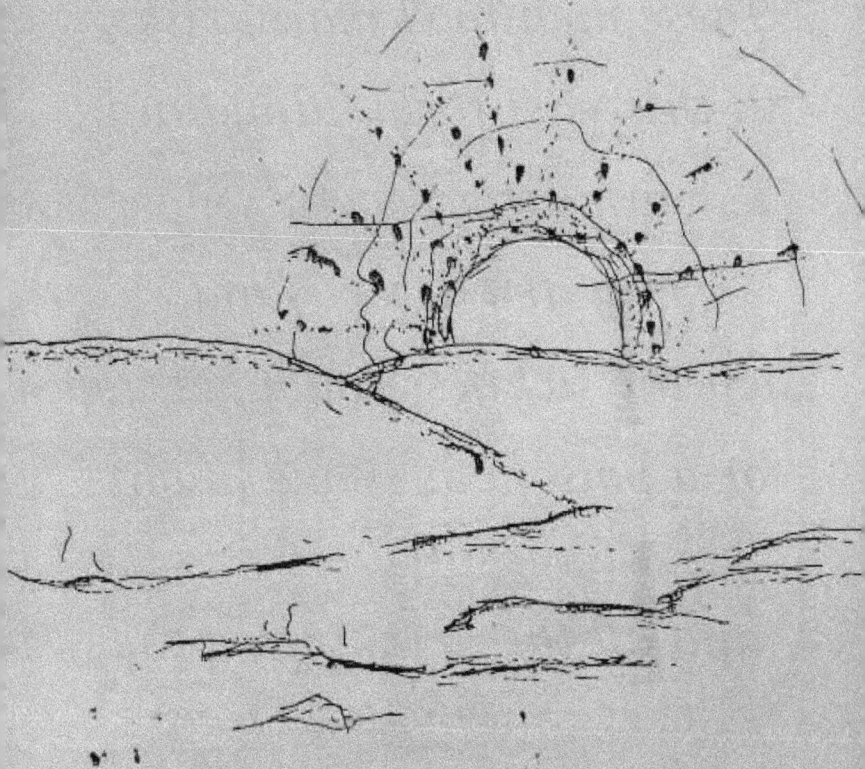

Warren Gatenby

These men took many risks,
in this vast forbidding land,
with little vegetation,
only dry desert sand.
Then the sickness could get you,
or a poisonous snake might
bite,
and all the drinking in the
pubs,
that usually ended in a fight.

Yet brave and resolute men,
were these prospectors of old,
hungrily pursuing,
this precious metal gold.
They held many grand visions,
of making some rich finds,
this one and only thought,
seemed to dominate their
minds.

Nama Goodey

Paddy Hannan struck it lucky,

in 1893,

on a low scrubland hill,

two companions and he.

Had stopped for the night,

and were camping in the bush,

having travelled from Coolgardie,

where there was a big goldrush.

Norman Gunston

Held up by a lame horse,

they had time to look around,

and many small gold nuggets,

were found there in the
ground.

They prospected further,

gathering 100 ounces all told,

of that much sought
treasure,

bright shiny gold.

SADDEN Gurchy.

Paddy rode back to Coolgardie,
to stake his new claim,
one that would result,
in bringing him much fame.
On the 15th June,
placed there for all to see,
his claim was nailed upon,
the trunk of a tree.

More than 1000 men followed,
Hannan's lucky find,
gold fever was on again,
few were left behind.
Yet soon it became known,
as a poor mans land,
because those miners couldn't dig,
that gold out just by hand.

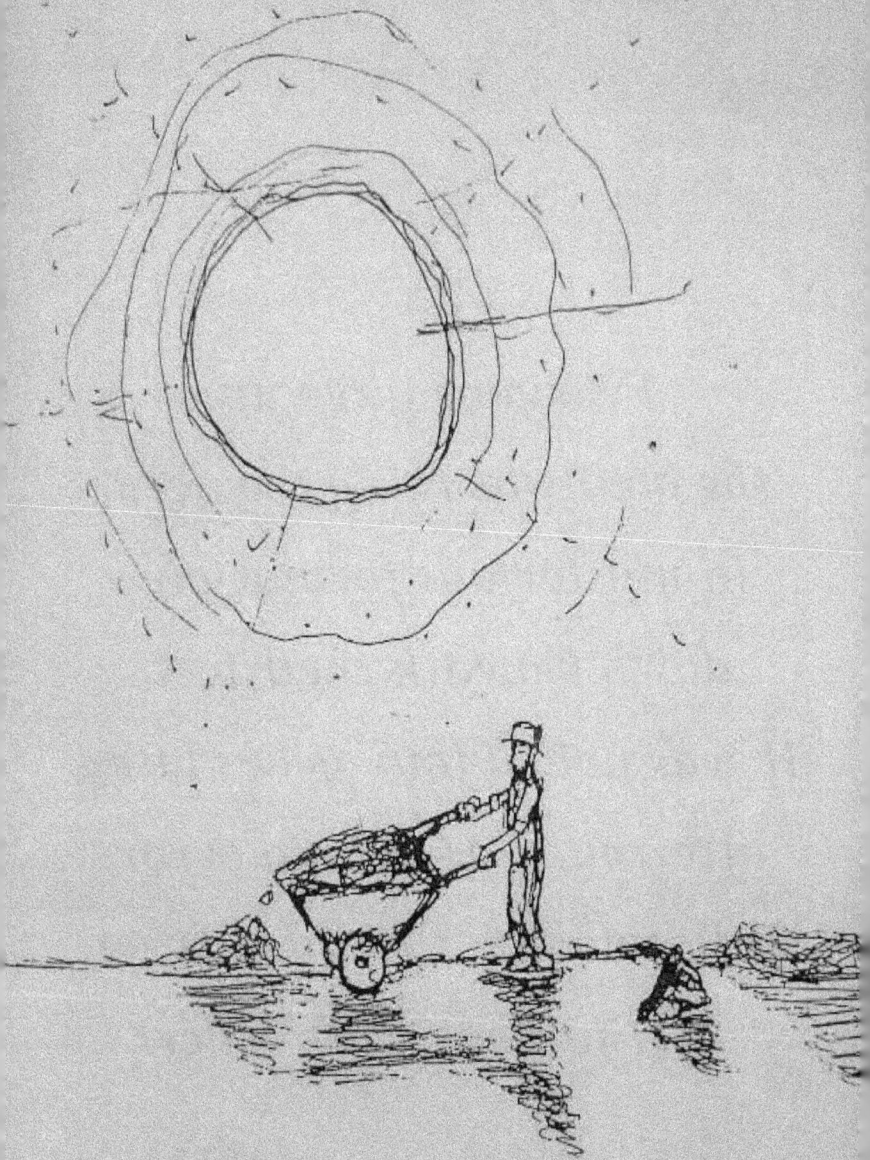

Warren Gunton

Everyone gave up,
the gold was lying too deep,
in mysterious formations,
down beneath their feet.
It was not til four years later,
after much trial and error,
did geologists finally extract,
that famous stuff yeller.

Warren Gunter

The mines then started,

Ivanhoe and Hannan's Star,

the richest square mile in the
world,

folk came in haste from near
and far.

So Kalgoorlie was born,

amidst homes of iron and
wood,

with hessian framed
structures,

and buildings stone and mud.

Warren Gundy

The town honoured Paddy,
a hero he became,
upon the rolls of time,
was written his name.

Success of the highest order,
had come to this quiet man,
who liked to roam the outback,
with his swag and billy can.

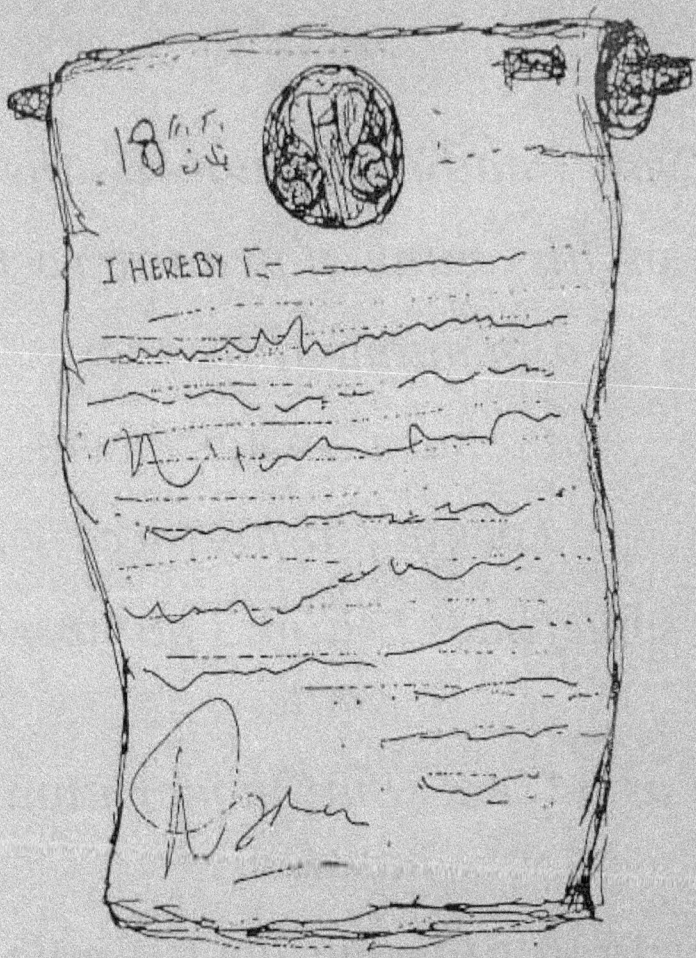

Now Paddy Hannan sits there,

on his chunk of granite rock,

a monument forever,

on a busy corner block.

Looking at his face,

sometimes I think I glimpse a
smile,

as he sees what modern man
has done,

to this famous golden mile.

man Gurty

About the Author

Esme has some wonderful stories to tell, from her days as a causality evacuation medic with the Royal Air Force to running boarding schools in outback Australia.

An active community member, volunteering as the first female to go on a live rescue in the wild Irish seas to dedicating years as a crisis telephone counsellor and Justice of the Peace.

Writing articles for local papers as well as writing historical ballads, children's stories and poems

Esme achieved a black belt in Karate when she was 58 years young and she went on to walk the Bibulmum track from end to end when she was 60 and for her 70th birthday became a pilgrim walking the Camino de Santiago trial in Spain.

Esme has delved into many writing genres, even doing a stint teaching creative writing in Esperance, Western Australia.

Esme celebrated her 54th wedding anniversary recently and has two daughters and a grandson.

Esme Kent

Brave volunteers . . .

Walker on track of something different

About the Illustrator

Warren Gundry is an artist living in Kalgoorlie/Boulder, he enjoyed working with Esme in 1988 when he was commissioned to illustrate the book.

Today Warren is still based in Kalgoorlie/Boulder and is known for his ceramic art.

Loveamore Other titles

Esme Kent has provided a fresh feel to motivation and inspiration with her book of sayings and quotes you can use to bring fresh perspectives to your day, to a situation or to a lift your spirits and provide that extra bounce in your step. In finding a new perspective, a different way of sharing a thought, a new outlook, an open mind, an inspired heart Esme has provided a path to finding re-invention in ourselves, finding magic, and ultimately weaving magic into our lives.

Weave Magic Into Your Life

by
Esme Kent

amazon

available to buy now
scan the QR code below

loveamore

A collection of poems from the soul for the soul, may words bring to life memories, feelings and emotions that move you, inspire you, ignite you as many moments have inspired this collection. With wonder we walk through the world, with sadness we see it's pain, with joy we experience it's beauty., with hope you will find beauty and inspiration in these words, from my heart to yours with love, peace and blessings.

Soul Collection

Victoria Kent

loveamore

Bonnie is a beautiful and loveable dog, she loves to say hello to people and she has many adventures meeting many new friends when she is out and about on her walks. Join Bonnie on her adventures meeting various animals showing the amazing wildlife you can see while just out walking in the suburbs of Quinns Rocks, Butler, Jindalee, Yanchep and Two Rocks in the State of Western Australia. The book uses real life photographs of Bonnie the dog meeting different animals, it is a fun story giving clues to each animal so the reader can guess what they are from the picture and verse.

loveamore Instagram

Socials

Follow
loveamore for
news of
upcoming
releases.

loveamore Facebook